CW01283998

The Book of Proverbs

God's Book of Wisdom

KJV (Simplified)

Edited by
Dr. Gerry D. Fox

All rights reserved.

ISBNs: 9798218033309 (hardcover), 9798218009120 (paperback), 9798218009137 (eBook)

This is the KJV (Simplified), replacing Old English with current English, current grammar, and current punctuation for quick, understandable reading. These updates were made by Dr. Gerry D. Fox.

Contents

My Story — vii

PART I
The Proverbs — 1

PART II
Three Simple Steps — 111

PART III
Final Thoughts — 115

My Story

My name is Dr. Gerry Fox. When I was sixteen and going through some challenges, my older sister told me I needed to read the book of Proverbs. She said, "Proverbs is considered GOD'S book of wisdom. There's thirty-one chapters, one for each day of the month. If you don't know what to read and it's the fourteenth, read the fourteenth chapter."

I thought I could at least read a chapter a day, and what I found was life changing. Proverbs is so packed with positive words of wisdom that it answered all my life's concerns and questions. When I was twenty-one, my father gave me a small pocket-size booklet titled *Living Proverbs*, and I carried it everywhere I went, reading it hundreds of times. Proverbs made such a powerful impact on my life that I wanted others to have the same experience, so I bought hundreds of them to give to my patients until the publisher stopped printing them. This compelled me to create a new booklet, and here it is. I hope you are able to gain as much insight from the book of Proverbs that I have and if you really want to experience the life-changing wisdom contained in

Proverbs, give copies of this booklet away. I truly believe you will see and experience the positive impact it has on others.

Part One

The Proverbs

Chapter 1

1 The proverbs of Solomon, the son of David, king of Israel;
2 To know wisdom and instruction; to perceive the words of understanding;
3 To receive the instruction of wisdom, justice, judgment, and equity;
4 To give subtlety to the simple, to the young man knowledge and discretion.
5 A wise *man* will hear and increase learning and a man of understanding shall listen to wise counsel;
6 To understand a proverb and the interpretation, the words of the wise and their dark sayings.
7 The fear of the LORD *is* the beginning of knowledge, *but* fools despise wisdom and instruction.
8 My son, hear the instruction of your father and forsake not the law of your mother;
9 For they *shall be* an ornament of grace to your head and chains on your neck.
10 My son, if sinners entice you, do not consent.

11 If they say, come with us, let us wait for blood, let us lurk privately for the innocent without cause;
12 Let us swallow them up alive as the grave, and whole, as those that go down into the pit.
13 We will find all precious substances; we shall fill our houses with spoil.
14 Cast in your lot among us; let us all have one purse.
15 My son, walk not in the way with them; refrain your foot from their path;
16 For their feet run to evil and make haste to shed blood.
17 Surely in vain the net is spread in the sight of any bird.
18 And they lie waiting for their *own* blood; they lurk privately for their *own* lives.
19 So *are* the ways of everyone that is greedy of gain, *which* takes away the life of the owners.
20 Wisdom cries out; she utters her voice in the streets;
21 She cries in the chief places of concourse, in the openings of the gates, in the city she utters her words, *saying,*
22 How long, you simple ones, will you love simplicity? And scorners delight in their scorning and fools hate knowledge?
23 Turn at my reproof; behold, I will pour out my spirit to you, and I will make my words known to you.
24 Because I have called and you refused, I have stretched out my hand and no one regarded.
25 But you have set at naught all my counsel and would have none of my reproof; therefore,
26 I will laugh at your calamity, and I will mock when your fear comes.
27 When your fear comes as desolation and your destruction comes as a whirlwind, when distress and anguish come upon you;

28 Then will you call upon me, but I will not answer. They shall seek me early, but they shall not find me.
29 For they hated knowledge and did not choose the fear of the LORD.
30 They would have none of my counsel, and they despised all my reproof.
31 Therefore, shall they eat of the fruit of their own way and be filled with their own devices.
32 For the turning away of the simple shall slay them, and the prosperity of fools shall destroy them.
33 But whoever hearkens unto me shall dwell safely and shall be quiet from fear of evil.

Chapter 2

1 My son, if you will receive my words and hide my commandments with you;
2 So that you incline your ear unto wisdom *and* apply your heart to understanding;
3 Yes, if you cry after knowledge *and* lift up your voice for understanding;
4 If you seek her as silver and search for her as *for* hidden treasures;
5 Then you shall understand the fear of the LORD and find the knowledge of God.
6 For the LORD gives wisdom; out of his mouth *comes* knowledge and understanding.
7 He lays up sound wisdom for the righteous; *He is* a buckler to them that walk uprightly.
8 He keeps the paths of judgment and preserves the way of his saints.
9 Then you will understand righteousness, judgment and equity; *yes*, every good path.
10 When wisdom enters into your heart, and knowledge is pleasant to your soul;

11 Discretion shall preserve you and understanding shall keep you;
12 To deliver you from the way of the evil *man*, from the man that speaks froward things;
13 Who leave the paths of uprightness, to walk in the ways of darkness;
14 Who rejoice to do evil *and* delight in the frowardness of the wicked;
15 Whose ways *are* crooked, and they froward in their paths;
16 To deliver you from the strange woman, *even* from the stranger who flatters with her words;
17 Who forsakes the guide of her youth and forgets the covenant of her God.
18 For her house inclines unto death and her paths unto the dead.
19 None that go into her return, neither will they take hold of the paths of life.
20 That you may walk in the way of good *men* and keep the paths of the righteous.
21 For the upright shall dwell in the land, and the perfect shall remain in it.
22 But the wicked shall be cut off from the earth, and the transgressors shall be rooted out of it.

Chapter 3

1 My son, forget not my law, but let your heart keep my commandments;
2 For length of days, long life, and peace shall they add to you.
3 Let not mercy and truth forsake you; bind them around your neck and write them upon the table of your heart:
4 So shall you find favor and good understanding in the sight of God and man.
5 Trust in the LORD with all your heart and lean not unto your own understanding.
6 In all your ways acknowledge Him, and He will direct your paths.
7 Be not wise in your own eyes; fear the LORD and depart from evil.
8 It shall be health to your navel and marrow to your bones.
9 Honor the LORD your substance and with the first fruits of all your increase:
10 So shall your barns be filled with plenty and your presses shall burst out with new wine.

11 My son, do not despise the chastening of the LORD; neither be weary of his correction;
12 For whom the LORD loves He corrects; even as a father the son *in whom* he delights.
13 Happy *is* the man *that* finds wisdom, and the man *that* gets understanding.
14 For the merchandise of it *is* better than the merchandise of silver and the gain than that of fine gold.
15 She *is* more precious than rubies, and all the things you can desire are not to be compared unto her.
16 Length of days *is* in her right hand, *and* in her left hand are riches and honor.
17 Her ways *are* ways of pleasantness, and all her paths *are* peace.
18 She *is* a tree of life to them that take hold of her, and happy *is everyone* who retains her.
19 The LORD by wisdom founded the earth; by understanding He established the heavens,
20 By His knowledge the depths are broken up and the clouds drop down the dew.
21 My son, don't let them depart from your eyes. Keep sound wisdom and discretion.
22 So shall they be life to your soul and grace to your neck.
23 Then shall you walk in your way safely, and your foot shall not stumble.
24 When you lie down, you shall not be afraid; yes, you shall lie down and your sleep shall be sweet.
25 Be not afraid of sudden fear, neither of the desolation of the wicked, when it comes.
26 For the LORD shall be your confidence and shall keep your foot from being taken.
27 Withhold not good from them to whom it is due, when it is in the power of your hand to do *it*.

28 Say not to your neighbor, "Go, and come again, and tomorrow I will give," when you have it by you.
29 Do not devise evil against your neighbor, seeing he dwells securely by you.
30 Strive not with a man without cause, if he has done you no harm.
31 Do not envy the oppressor and choose none of his ways;
32 For the froward *is* an abomination to the LORD: but His secret *is* with the righteous.
33 The curse of the LORD *is* in the house of the wicked, but He blesses the habitation of the just.
34 Surely, He scorns the scorners, but He gives grace unto the lowly.
35 The wise shall inherit glory, but shame shall be the promotion of fools.

Chapter 4

1 Hear, you children, the instruction of a father and attend to know understanding,
2 For I give you good doctrine; forsake not my law.
3 For I was my father's son, tender and only *beloved* in the sight of my mother.
4 He taught me and said, let your heart retain my words, keep my commandments and live.
5 Get wisdom, get understanding, and do not forget *it*; do not decline from the words of my mouth.
6 Forsake her not, and she will preserve you; love her and she will keep you.
7 Wisdom *is* the principal thing; *therefore*, get wisdom, and with all your getting, get understanding.
8 Exalt her, and she shall promote you; she shall bring you to honor when you embrace her.
9 She shall give to your head an ornament of grace, and a crown of glory shall she deliver to you.
10 Hear, O my son, and receive my sayings; and the years of your life shall be many.

11 I have taught you in the way of wisdom; I have led you in the right paths.
12 When you go, your steps shall not be straightened; and when you run, you shall not stumble.
13 Take fast hold of instruction, let *her* not go and keep her; for she *is* your life.
14 Enter not into the path of the wicked and go not in the way of evil *men*.
15 Avoid it, pass not by it, turn from it, and pass away.
16 For they sleep not, except they have done mischief; and their sleep is taken away, unless they cause *some* to fall.
17 For they eat the bread of wickedness and drink the wine of violence.
18 But the path of the just *is* as the shining light, that shines more and more unto the perfect day.
19 The way of the wicked *is* as darkness; they know not at what they stumble.
20 My son, attend to my words; incline your ear unto my sayings.
21 Let them not depart from your eyes; keep them in the midst of your heart.
22 For they *are* life to those who find them and health to all their flesh.
23 Keep your heart with all diligence, for out of it *are* the issues of life.
24 Put away from you a froward mouth, and perverse lips put far from you.
25 Let your eyes look right on, and let your eyelids look straight before you.
26 Ponder the path of your feet, and let all your ways be established.
27 Turn not to the right hand nor to the left, and remove your foot from evil.

Chapter 5

1 My son, attend unto my wisdom *and* bow your ear to my understanding:
2 That you may regard discretion and your lips may keep knowledge.
3 For the lips of a strange woman drop *as* a honeycomb, and her mouth *is* smoother than oil;
4 But her end is bitter as wormwood, sharp as a two-edged sword.
5 Her feet go down to death; her steps take hold on hell.
6 Lest you should ponder the path of life, her ways are moveable, *that* you cannot know *them*.
7 Hear me now, therefore, O ye children, and depart not from the words of my mouth.
8 Remove your way far from her and come not near the door of her house;
9 Lest you give your honor unto others and your years unto the cruel;
10 Lest strangers be filled with your wealth and your labors *be* in the house of a stranger;

11 And you mourn at the last, when your flesh and your body are consumed,
12 And say, how have I hated instruction and my heart despised reproof;
13 And have not obeyed the voice of my teachers, nor inclined my ear to them that instructed me!
14 I was almost in all evil in the midst of the congregation and assembly.
15 Drink water out of your own cistern and running water out of your own well.
16 Let your fountains be dispersed abroad *and* rivers of water in the streets.
17 Let them be only your own and not for strangers with you.
18 Let your fountain be blessed and rejoice with the wife of your youth.
19 *Let her be as* the loving hind and pleasant roe, let her breasts always satisfy you and always be ravished with her love.
20 And why will you, my son, be ravished with a strange woman and embrace the bosom of a stranger?
21 For the ways of man *are* before the eyes of the LORD, and He ponders all his goings.
22 His own iniquities shall take the wicked himself, and he shall be held with the cords of his sins.
23 He shall die without instruction, and in the greatness of his folly he shall go astray.

Chapter 6

1 My son, if you are surety for your friend, *if* you have shaken your hand with a stranger,
2 You are snared with the words of your mouth; you are taken with the words of your mouth.
3 Do this now, my son, and deliver yourself, when you come into the hand of your friend; go, humble yourself and make sure your friend.
4 Give not sleep to your eyes, nor slumber to your eyelids.
5 Deliver yourself as a roe from the hand *of the hunter* and as a bird from the hand of the fowler.
6 Go to the ant, you sluggard; consider her ways and be wise;
7 Which having no guide, overseer or ruler,
8 Provides her meat in the summer and gathers her food in the harvest.
9 How long will you sleep, O sluggard? When will you arise out of your sleep?
10 *A* little sleep, a little slumber, a little folding of the hands to sleep;

11 So shall your poverty come as one that travels and your want as an armed man.
12 A naughty person, a wicked man, walks with a froward mouth.
13 He winks with his eyes, he speaks with his feet, and he teaches with his fingers.
14 Frowardness *is* in his heart; he devises mischief continually; he spreads discord.
15 Therefore shall his calamity come suddenly; suddenly shall he be broken without remedy.
16 These six *things* do the LORD hate: yes, seven *are* an abomination unto him:
17 A proud look, a lying tongue, and hands that shed innocent blood,
18 A heart that devises wicked imaginations, feet that are swift in running to mischief,
19 A false witness *that* speaks lies and spreads discord among brethren.
20 My son, keep your father's commandment and forsake not the law of your mother.
21 Bind them continually upon your heart and tie them around your neck.
22 When you go, it will lead you; when you sleep, it will keep you; and *when* you awaken, it will talk with you.
23 For the commandment *is* a lamp, the law *is* light, and reproofs of instruction *are* the way of life;
24 To keep you from the evil woman, from the flattery of the tongue of a strange woman.
25 Lust not after her beauty in your heart, neither let her take you with her eyelids;
26 For by means of a whorish woman *a man is brought* to a piece of bread, and the adulteress will hunt for the precious life.

27 Can a man take fire in his bosom and his clothes not be burned?
28 Can one walk upon hot coals and his feet not be burned?
29 So is he who goes into his neighbor's wife; whosoever touches her shall not be innocent.
30 *Men* do not despise a thief, if he steals to satisfy his soul when he is hungry.
31 But *if* he is found, he will restore sevenfold; he will give all the substance of his house.
32 Whoever commits adultery lacks understanding and destroys his own soul.
33 A wound and dishonor shall he get, and his reproach shall not be wiped away;
34 For jealousy *is* the rage of a man, and he will not spare in the day of vengeance.
35 He will not regard any ransom, nor will he rest content, though you give many gifts.

Chapter 7

1 My son, keep my words and hold my commandments with you.
2 Keep my commandments and live. Keep my law as the apple of your eye.
3 Bind them upon your fingers and write them upon the table of your heart.
4 Say unto wisdom, you *are* my sister and call understanding your kinswoman;
5 That they may keep you from the strange woman, from the stranger *who* flatters with her words.
6 For at the window of my house, I looked through my casement,
7 And beheld among the simple ones, I discerned among the youths, a young man lacking understanding,
8 Passing through the street near her corner, and he went the way to her house,
9 In the twilight, in the evening, in the black and dark night;
10 And, behold, there met him a woman *dressed like* a harlot, and she was subtle of heart.

11 (She *is* loud, stubborn, and her feet abide not in her house.
12 Now *is she* out in the streets and lies waiting at every corner.)
13 So she caught him, kissed him, *and* with an impudent face said unto him,
14 *I have* peace offerings with me. This day have I paid my vows.
15 Therefore, I came out to meet you, diligently to seek your face, and I have found you.
16 I have decked my bed with coverings of tapestry, with carved *works* and fine linen of Egypt.
17 I have perfumed my bed with myrrh, aloe, and cinnamon.
18 Come, let us take our fill of love until the morning. Let us solace ourselves with love.
19 For the goodman *is* not at home; he has gone on a long journey.
20 He has taken a bag of money with him and will come home on the appointed day.
21 With her much fair speech she caused him to yield, with the flattering of her lips she forced him.
22 He goes after her straightway, as an ox goes to the slaughter, or as a fool to the correction of the stocks;
23 Till a dart strikes through his liver; as a bird hastens to the snare and knows not that it *is* for his life.
24 Hearken unto me now, therefore, O you children, and attend to the words of my mouth.
25 Let not your heart decline to her ways nor go astray in her paths.
26 For she has cast down many wounded; yes, many strong *men* have been slain by her.
27 Her house *is* the way to hell, going down to the chambers of death.

Chapter 8

1 Does not wisdom cry and understanding put forth her voice?
2 She stands in the top of high places, in the places of the paths.
3 She cries at the gates, at the entry of the city, and at the coming in at the doors.
4 Unto you, O men, I call, and my voice *is* to the sons of man.
5 O you simple, understand wisdom, and you fools be of an understanding heart.
6 Hear, for I will speak of excellent things, and the opening of my lips *speak* right things.
7 For my mouth shall speak truth, and wickedness *is* an abomination to my lips.
8 All the words of my mouth *are* in righteousness; *there is* nothing froward or perverse in them.
9 They *are* all plain to him that understands and right to them that find knowledge.
10 Receive my instruction, and not silver, and knowledge rather than choice gold.

11 For wisdom *is* better than rubies, and all the things that may be desired are not to be compared to it.
12 I, wisdom, dwell with prudence and find out knowledge of witty inventions.
13 The fear of the LORD *is* to hate evil, pride, arrogance, and the evil way, and the froward mouth, do I hate.
14 Counsel and sound wisdom *is* mine. I *am* understanding, and I have strength.
15 By me kings reign and princes decree justice.
16 By me princes and nobles rule, *even* all the judges of the earth.
17 I love them that love me, and those that seek me early shall find me.
18 Riches and honor *are* with me; *yes*, durable riches and righteousness.
19 My fruit *is* better than gold, yes, than fine gold, and my revenue is better than choice silver.
20 I lead in the way of righteousness, amid the paths of judgment;
21 That I may cause those that love me to inherit substance, and I will fill their treasuries.
22 The LORD possessed me in the beginning of His way, before His works of old.
23 I was set up from everlasting, from the beginning, or ever the earth was.
24 When *there were* no depths, I was brought forth, when *there were* no fountains abounding with water.
25 Before the mountains were settled, before the hills, I was brought forth;
26 While yet He had not made the earth, nor the fields, nor the highest part of the dust of the world.
27 When He prepared the heavens and set a compass upon the face of the depth, I *was* there.

28 When He established the clouds above, when He strengthened the fountains of the deep,

29 When He gave to the sea His decree, that the waters should not pass His commandment, when He appointed the foundations of the earth;

30 Then I was by Him, *as* one brought up *with Him*; and I was daily *His* delight, rejoicing always before Him;

31 Rejoicing in the habitable part of His earth; and my delights *were* with the sons of men.

32 Now, therefore, listen to me, O ye children, for blessed *are they that* keep my ways.

33 Hear instruction, be wise, and refuse it not.

34 Blessed *is* the man that hears me, watching daily at my gates and waiting at the posts of my doors.

35 For whoever finds me finds life and shall obtain favor of the LORD.

36 But he who sins against me wrongs his own soul. All those who hate me love death.

Chapter 9

1 Wisdom has built her house and has hewn out her seven pillars.
2 She has killed her beasts; she has mingled her wine; she has also furnished her table.
3 She has sent forth her maidens. She cries upon the highest places of the city;
4 Whoever *is* simple, let him turn in here. *As for* him who wants understanding, she says to him,
5 Come, eat of my bread and drink of the wine I have mingled.
6 Forsake the foolish and live. Go in the way of understanding.
7 He that reproves a scorner gets shame, and he that rebukes a wicked *man gets a* blot.
8 Reprove not a scorner, lest he hate you; rebuke a wise man and he will love you.
9 Give *instruction* to a wise *man* and he will be yet wiser; teach a just *man* and he will increase in learning.
10 The fear of the LORD *is* the beginning of wisdom, and the knowledge of the Holy One *is* understanding.

11 For by me your days shall be multiplied and the years of your life shall be increased.
12 If you are wise, you are wise for yourself; but *if* you scorn, you alone shall bear *it*.
13 A foolish woman *is* clamorous. *She is* simple and knows nothing.
14 For she sits at the door of her house, on a seat in the high places of the city,
15 Calling to those who go right on their way.
16 Whoever *is* simple, let him turn in here; and *as for* him who wants understanding, she says to him,
17 Stolen waters are sweet and bread *eaten* in secret is pleasant.
18 But he knows not that the dead *are* there *and that* her guests *are* in the depths of hell.

Chapter 10

1 The proverbs of Solomon. A wise son makes a glad father, but a foolish son *is* the heaviness of his mother.
2 Treasures of wickedness profit nothing, but righteousness delivers from death.
3 The LORD will not suffer the soul of the righteous to famish but he casts away the substance of the wicked.
4 He becomes poor that deals *with* a slack hand, but the hand of the diligent makes rich.
5 He that gathers in summer *is* a wise son, *but* he that sleeps in harvest *is* a son that causes shame.
6 Blessings *are* upon the head of the just, but violence covers the mouth of the wicked.
7 The memory of the just *is* blessed, but the name of the wicked shall rot.
8 The wise in heart will receive commandments, but a chattering fool will fall.
9 He that walks uprightly walks surely, but he that perverts his ways shall be known.
10 He that winks with the eye causes sorrow, but a chattering fool will fall.

11 The mouth of a righteous *man is* a well of life, but violence covers the mouth of the wicked.
12 Hatred stirs up strife, but love covers all sins.
13 In the lips of him that has understanding, wisdom is found, but a rod *is* for the back of him that is void of understanding.
14 Wise *men* preserve knowledge, but the mouth of the foolish *is* near destruction.
15 The rich man's wealth *is* his strong city; the destruction of the poor *is* their poverty.
16 The labor of the righteous *tends* to life; the fruit of the wicked to sin.
17 He *is in* the way of life that keeps instruction, but he that refuses reproof errs.
18 He that hides hatred *with* lying lips, and he that utters a slander *is* a fool.
19 In the multitude of words there lacks not sin, but he that refrains his lips *is* wise.
20 The tongue of the just *is as* choice silver; the heart of the wicked *is* of little worth.
21 The lips of the righteous feed many, but fools die for lack of wisdom.
22 The blessing of the LORD makes rich, and he adds no sorrow with it.
23 *It is* like sport to a fool to do mischief, but a man of understanding has wisdom.
24 The fear of the wicked shall come upon him, but the desire of the righteous shall be granted.
25 As the whirlwind passes, so *is* the wicked no *more*; but the righteous *is* an everlasting foundation.
26 As vinegar to the teeth and smoke to the eyes, so *is* the sluggard to them that send him.
27 The fear of the LORD prolongs days, but the years of the wicked shall be shortened.

28 The hope of the righteous *shall be* gladness, but the expectation of the wicked shall perish.

29 The way of the LORD *is* strength to the upright, but destruction *shall be* to the workers of iniquity.

30 The righteous shall never be removed, and the wicked shall not inhabit the earth.

31 The mouth of the just brings forth wisdom, but the froward tongue shall be cut out.

32 The lips of the righteous know what is acceptable, but the mouth of the wicked *speaks* perverseness.

Chapter 11

1 A false balance *is* an abomination to the LORD, but a just weight *is* his delight.
2 *When* pride comes, then comes shame, but with the lowly *is* wisdom.
3 The integrity of the upright shall guide them, but the perverseness of transgressors shall destroy them.
4 Riches profit not in the day of wrath, but righteousness delivers from death.
5 The righteousness of the perfect shall direct his way, but the wicked shall fall by his own wickedness.
6 The righteousness of the upright shall deliver them, but transgressors shall be taken in *their own* iniquity.
7 When a wicked man dies, *his* expectation shall perish, and the hope of unjust *men* perishes.
8 The righteous are delivered out of trouble, and the wicked come in his stead.
9 A hypocrite with *his* mouth destroys his neighbor, but through knowledge shall the just be delivered.
10 When it goes well with the righteous, the city rejoices; and when the wicked perish, *there is* shouting.

11 By the blessing of the upright, the city is exalted, but it is overthrown by the mouth of the wicked.
12 He that is void of wisdom despises his neighbor, but a man of understanding holds his peace.
13 A talebearer reveals secrets, but he that has a faithful spirit conceals the matter.
14 Where there is no counsel, the people fall but in the multitude of counselors *there is* safety.
15 He that is surety for a stranger will smart *for it*, and he that hates suretyship is sure.
16 A gracious woman retains honor, and strong *men* retain riches.
17 The merciful man does good to his own soul, but *he that is* cruel troubles his own flesh.
18 The wicked work a deceitful work, but to him that spreads righteousness *shall be* a sure reward.
19 As righteousness *tends* to life so, he that pursues evil *pursues it* to his own death.
20 They that are of a perverse heart *are* an abomination to the LORD, but *such as are* upright in *their* way *are* his delight.
21 *Though* hand *joins* in hand, the wicked shall not be unpunished; but the seed of the righteous shall be delivered.
22 *As* a jewel of gold in a swine's snout, *so is* a fair woman who is without discretion.
23 The desire of the righteous *is* only good; *but* the expectation of the wicked *is* wrath.
24 There are those that scatter, and yet increase and *there are those* that withhold more than is needed, but *it leads* to poverty.
25 The liberal soul shall be made fat, and he that waters shall be watered also himself.

26 He that withholds grain, the people shall curse him but blessings *shall be* upon the head of him that sells *it*.

27 He that diligently seeks good procures favor, but he that seeks mischief, it shall come unto him.

28 He that trusts in his riches shall fall, but the righteous shall flourish as a branch.

29 He that troubles his own house shall inherit the wind, and the fool *shall be* servant to the wise of heart.

30 The fruit of the righteous *is* a tree of life, and he that wins souls *is* wise.

31 Behold, the righteous shall be recompensed in the earth, much more the wicked and the sinner.

Chapter 12

1 Whoever loves instruction loves knowledge, but he that hates reproof *is* stupid.
2 A good *man* obtains favor of the LORD, but a man of wicked devices will He condemn.
3 A man shall not be established by wickedness, but the root of the righteous shall not be moved.
4 A virtuous woman *is* a crown to her husband, but she that makes ashamed *is* as rottenness in his bones.
5 The thoughts of the righteous *are* right, *but* the counsels of the wicked *are* deceit.
6 The words of the wicked *are* to lie in wait for blood, but the mouth of the upright shall deliver them.
7 The wicked are overthrown, and *are* not, but the house of the righteous shall stand.
8 A man shall be commended according to his wisdom, but he that is of a perverse heart shall be despised.
9 *He that is* despised, and has a servant, *is* better than he that honors himself and lacks bread.
10 A righteous *man* regards the life of his beast, but the tender mercies of the wicked *are* cruel.

11 He that tills his land shall be satisfied with bread, but he that follows vain *persons is* void of understanding.
12 The wicked desire the net of evil *men*, but the root of the righteous yields *fruit*.
13 The wicked is snared by the transgression of *his* lips, but the just shall come out of trouble.
14 A man shall be satisfied with good by the fruit of *his* mouth, and the recompence of a man's hands shall be rendered unto him.
15 The way of a fool *is* right in his own eyes, but he that hearkens unto counsel *is* wise.
16 A fool's wrath is presently known, but a prudent *man* covers shame.
17 *He that* speaks truth shows righteousness but a false witness, deceit.
18 There is he that speaks like the piercings of a sword, but the tongue of the wise *is* health.
19 The lip of truth shall be established forever, but a lying tongue *is* but for a moment.
20 Deceit *is* in the heart of them that imagine evil, but to the counselors of peace *is* joy.
21 There shall no evil happen to the just, but the wicked will be filled with mischief.
22 Lying lips *are* an abomination to the LORD, but they that deal truly *are* his delight.
23 A prudent man conceals knowledge, but the hearts of fools proclaim foolishness.
24 The hand of the diligent shall bear rule, but the slothful will be put to forced labor.
25 Heaviness in the heart of man makes it stoop, but a good word makes it glad.
26 The righteous *is* more excellent than his neighbor, but the way of the wicked seduces them.

27 The slothful *man* roasts not that which he took in hunting, but the substance of a diligent man *is* precious.
28 In the way of righteousness *is* life and, in their pathway, *there is* no death.

Chapter 13

1 A wise son *hears* his father's instruction, but a scorner hears not rebuke.
2 A man shall eat good by the fruit of *his* mouth but the souls of the transgressors *shall eat* violence.
3 He that keeps his mouth keeps his life, *but* he that opens wide his lips shall have destruction.
4 The soul of the sluggard desires and *has* nothing, but the soul of the diligent shall be made fat.
5 A righteous *man* hates lying, but a wicked *man* is loathsome and comes to shame.
6 Righteousness keeps *him that is* upright in the way, but wickedness overthrows the sinner.
7 There is he that makes himself rich yet *has* nothing, and *there is* he that makes himself poor yet *has* great riches.
8 The ransom of a man's life *is* his riches, but the poor hears not rebuke.
9 The light of the righteous rejoices, but the lamp of the wicked shall be put out.
10 Only by pride comes contention, but with the well advised *is* wisdom.

11 Wealth gained by vanity shall be diminished, but he that gathers by labor shall increase.
12 Hope deferred makes the heart sick, but *when* the desire comes *it is* a tree of life.
13 Whoever despises the word shall be destroyed, but he that fears the commandment shall be rewarded.
14 The law of the wise *is* a fountain of life, to depart from the snares of death.
15 Good understanding gives favor, but the way of transgressors *is* hard.
16 Every prudent *man* deals with knowledge, but a fool lays open *his* folly.
17 A wicked messenger falls into mischief, but a faithful ambassador *is* health.
18 Poverty and shame *shall be to* him that refuses instruction, but he that regards reproof shall be honored.
19 The desire accomplished is sweet to the soul, but *it is* an abomination to fools to depart from evil.
20 He that walks with wise *men* shall be wise, but a companion of fools shall be destroyed.
21 Evil pursues sinners, but to the righteous good shall be repaid.
22 A good *man* leaves an inheritance to his children's children, and the wealth of the sinner *is* laid up for the just.
23 Much food *is in* the tillage of the poor, but there is he *that is* destroyed for lack of judgment.
24 He that spares his rod hates his son, but he that loves him chastens him early.
25 The righteous eats to the satisfying of his soul, but the belly of the wicked shall want.

Chapter 14

1 Every wise woman builds her house, but the foolish plucks it down with her hands.
2 He that walks in his uprightness fears the LORD, but *he that is* perverse in his ways despises Him.
3 In the mouth of the foolish *is* a rod of pride, but the lips of the wise shall preserve them.
4 Where no oxen *are*, the crib *is* clean, but much increase *is* by the strength of the ox.
5 A faithful witness will not lie, but a false witness will utter lies.
6 A scorner seeks wisdom and *finds it* not, but knowledge *is* easy to him that understands.
7 Go from the presence of a foolish man, when you perceive not *in him* the lips of knowledge.
8 The wisdom of the prudent *is* to understand his way, but the folly of fools *is* deceit.
9 Fools make a mock at sin, but among the righteous *there is* favor.
10 The heart knows its own bitterness and a stranger does not meddle with its joy.

11 The house of the wicked shall be overthrown, but the tabernacle of the upright shall flourish.
12 There is a way which seems right unto a man, but the end thereof, *are* the ways of death.
13 Even in laughter the heart is sorrowful, and the end of that mirth *is* heaviness.
14 The backslider in heart shall be filled with his own ways, and a good man *shall be satisfied* from himself.
15 The simple believe every word, but the prudent *man* looks well to his going.
16 A wise *man* fears and departs from evil, but the fool rages and is confident.
17 *He that is* soon angry deals foolishly, and a man of wicked devices is hated.
18 The simple inherit folly, but the prudent are crowned with knowledge.
19 The evil bow before the good, and the wicked bow at the gates of the righteous.
20 The poor are hated even by their own neighbors, but the rich *have* many friends.
21 He that despises his neighbor, sins, but he that has mercy on the poor is happy.
22 Do they not err that devise evil? But mercy and truth *shall be* to them that devise good.
23 In all labor there is profit, but the talk of the lips *leads* only to poverty.
24 The crown of the wise *is* their riches, *but* the foolishness of fools *is* folly.
25 A true witness delivers souls, but a deceitful *witness* speaks lies.
26 In the fear of the LORD *is* strong confidence, and His children shall have a place of refuge.
27 The fear of the LORD *is* a fountain of life, to depart from the snares of death.

28 In the multitude of people *is* a king's honor, but in the lack of people *is* the destruction of a prince.
29 *He that is* slow to wrath *is* of great understanding, but *he that is* hasty of spirit exalts folly.
30 A sound heart *is* the life of the flesh, but envy is the rottenness of the bones.
31 He that oppresses the poor reproaches his Maker, but he that honors Him has mercy on the poor.
32 The wicked is driven away in his wickedness, but the righteous has hope in his death.
33 Wisdom rests in the heart of him who has understanding, but *that which is in the* midst of fools is made known.
34 Righteousness exalts a nation, but sin *is* a reproach to any people.
35 The king's favor *is* toward a wise servant, but his wrath is *against* him that causes shame.

Chapter 15

1 A soft answer turns away wrath, but grievous words stir up anger.
2 The tongue of the wise uses knowledge aright, but the mouth of fools pours out foolishness.
3 The eyes of the LORD *are* in every place watching the evil and the good.
4 A wholesome tongue *is* a tree of life, but perverseness *is* a breach in the spirit.
5 A fool despises his father's instruction, but he that regards reproof is prudent.
6 In the house of the righteous *is* much treasure, but in the revenues of the wicked is trouble.
7 The lips of the wise disperse knowledge, but the heart of fools *does* not.
8 The sacrifice of the wicked *is* an abomination to the LORD, but the prayer of the upright *is* his delight.
9 The way of the wicked *is* an abomination unto the LORD, but He loves him that follows after righteousness.

10 Correction *is* grievous unto him that forsakes the way, *and* he that hates reproof shall die.
11 Hell and destruction *are* before the LORD, so how much more the hearts of the children of men?
12 A scorner loves not one that reproves him, neither will he go unto the wise.
13 A merry heart makes a cheerful countenance, but by sorrow of the heart the spirit is broken.
14 The heart of him that has understanding seeks knowledge, but the mouth of fools feeds on foolishness.
15 All the days of the afflicted *are* evil, but he that is of a merry heart *has* a continual feast.
16 Better *is* little with the fear of the LORD than great treasure and trouble therewith.
17 Better *is* a dinner of herbs, where love is, than a stalled ox with hatred.
18 A wrathful man stirs up strife, but *he that is* slow to anger appeases strife.
19 The way of the slothful *man is* as a hedge of thorns, but the way of the righteous *is* made plain.
20 A wise son makes a glad father, but a foolish man despises his mother.
21 Folly *is* joy to *him that is* destitute of wisdom, but a man of understanding walks uprightly.
22 Without counsel purposes are disappointed, but in the multitude of counselors they are established.
23 A man has joy by the answer of his mouth, and a word *spoken* in due season, how good it is!
24 The way of life *is* above to the wise, that he may depart from hell beneath.
25 The LORD will destroy the house of the proud, but he will establish the border of the widow.
26 The thoughts of the wicked *are* an abomination to the LORD, but *the words* of the pure *are* pleasant.

27 He that is greedy of gain troubles his own house, but he that hates gifts shall live.

28 The heart of the righteous studies how to answer, but the mouth of the wicked pours out evil things.

29 The LORD *is* far from the wicked, but He hears the prayer of the righteous.

30 The light of the eyes rejoices the heart, *and* a good report makes the bones fat.

31 The ear that hears the reproofs of life abides among the wise.

32 He that refuses instruction despises his own soul, but he that hears reproof gets understanding.

33 The fear of the LORD *is* the instruction of wisdom, and before honor *is* humility.

Chapter 16

1 The preparations of the heart belong to man, and the answer of the tongue *is* from the LORD.
2 All the ways of a man *are* clean in his own eyes, but the LORD weighs the spirits.
3 Commit your works unto the LORD, and your thoughts shall be established.
4 The LORD made all *things* for himself, yes, even the wicked for the day of evil.
5 Everyone *that is* proud in heart *is* an abomination to the LORD; *though* hand *join* in hand, he shall not go unpunished.
6 By mercy and truth iniquity is purged, and by the fear of the LORD, *men* depart from evil.
7 When a man's ways please the LORD, he makes even his enemies to be at peace with him.
8 Better *is* a little with righteousness than great revenues without right.
9 A man's heart devises his way, but the LORD directs his steps.

10 A divine sentence *is* in the lips of the king, and his mouth transgresses not in judgment.
11 A just weight and balance *are* the LORD'S; all the weights of the bag *are* His work.
12 *It is* an abomination to kings to commit wickedness for the throne is established by righteousness.
13 Righteous lips *are* the delight of kings, and they love him that speaks right.
14 The wrath of a king *is as* messengers of death, but a wise man will pacify it.
15 In the light of the king's countenance *is* life, and his favor *is* like a cloud of the latter rain.
16 How much better *it is* to get wisdom than gold, and to get understanding is to be chosen rather than silver!
17 The highway of the upright *is* to depart from evil; he that keeps his way preserves his soul.
18 Pride *goes* before destruction and a haughty spirit before a fall.
19 Better *it is to be* of a humble spirit with the lowly than to divide the spoil with the proud.
20 He that handles a matter wisely shall find good, and whoever trusts in the LORD is happy.
21 The wise in heart shall be called prudent, and the sweetness of the lips increases learning.
22 Understanding *is* a wellspring of life to him that has it, but the instruction of fools *is* folly.
23 The heart of the wise teaches his mouth and adds learning to his lips.
24 Pleasant words *are like a* honeycomb, sweet to the soul and health to the bones.
25 There is a way that seems right unto a man, but the end thereof, *is* the way of death.
26 He that labors, labors for himself, for his mouth craves it of him.

27 An ungodly man digs up evil, and in his lips *there is a* burning fire.
28 A perverse man sows strife, and a whisperer separates chief friends.
29 A violent man entices his neighbor and leads him into a way *that is* not good.
30 He shuts his eyes to devise froward things, and moving his lips he brings evil to pass.
31 The hoary head *is* a crown of glory *if* it is found in the way of righteousness.
32 *He that is* slow to anger *is* better than the mighty, and he that rules his own spirit than he that takes a city.
33 The lot is cast into the lap, but the whole disposing thereof *is* of the LORD.

Chapter 17

1 Better *is* a dry morsel with quietness than a house full of sacrifices *with* strife.
2 A wise servant shall have rule over a son that causes shame and shall have part of the inheritance among the brethren.
3 The fining pot *is* for silver and the furnace for gold, but the LORD tries the hearts.
4 A wicked doer gives heed to false lips, *and* a liar gives ear to a mischievous tongue.
5 Whoever mocks the poor reproaches his Maker, *and* he that is glad at calamities shall not go unpunished.
6 Children's children *are* the crown of old men, and the glory of children *are* their fathers.
7 Excellent speech becomes not a fool, much less do lying lips a prince.
8 A gift *is* a precious stone in the eyes of him who has it, and wherever it turns, it prospers.
9 He that covers a transgression seeks love, but he that repeats a matter separates *very* friends.

10 A reproof enters more into a wise man than a hundred stripes into a fool.
11 An evil *man* seeks only rebellion; therefore, a cruel messenger shall be sent against him.
12 Let a bear robbed of her whelps meet a man rather than a fool in his folly.
13 Whoever rewards evil for good, evil shall not depart from his house.
14 The beginning of strife *is like* when one lets out water; therefore, leave off contention before it is meddled with.
15 He that justifies the wicked and he that condemns the just *are* both an abomination to the LORD.
16 Why *is there* a price in the hand of a fool to get wisdom, seeing *he has* no heart *to it?*
17 A friend loves at all times, and a brother is born for adversity.
18 A man void of understanding strikes hands *and* becomes surety in the presence of his friend.
19 He loves transgression that loves strife, *and* he that exalts his gate seeks destruction.
20 He that has a froward heart finds no good, and he that has a perverse tongue falls into mischief.
21 He that begets a fool *does it* to his sorrow, and the father of a fool has no joy.
22 A merry heart does good *like* a medicine, but a broken spirit dries the bones.
23 A wicked *man* takes a gift out of the bosom to pervert the ways of judgment.
24 Wisdom *is* before him that has understanding, but the eyes of a fool *are* on the ends of the earth.
25 A foolish son *is* a grief to his father and bitterness to her that bore him.

26 To punish the just *is* not good *nor* to strike princes for their equity.
27 He that has knowledge spares his words, *and* a man of understanding is of an excellent spirit.
28 Even a fool, when he holds his peace, is counted wise, *and* he that shuts his lips *is esteemed* a man of understanding.

Chapter 18

1 Through desire a man, having separated himself, seeks *and* intermeddles with all wisdom.
2 A fool has no delight in understanding, but that his heart may discover itself.
3 When the wicked comes, *then* also comes contempt, and with dishonor, disgrace.
4 The words of a man's mouth *are as* deep waters *and* the wellspring of wisdom, *as* a flowing brook.
5 *It is* not good to accept the person of the wicked or to overthrow the righteous in judgment.
6 A fool's lips enter into contention, and his mouth calls for strokes.
7 A fool's mouth *is* his destruction, and his lips *are* the snare of his soul.
8 The words of a talebearer *are* like wounds, and they go down into the innermost parts of the belly.
9 He that is slothful in his work is brother to him that is a great waster.
10 The name of the LORD *is* a strong tower; the righteous run into it and are safe.

11 The rich man's wealth *is* his strong city and like a high wall in his own conceit.
12 Before destruction the heart of man is haughty, and before honor *is* humility.
13 He that answers a matter before he hears *it*, it *is* folly and shame unto him.
14 The spirit of a man will sustain his infirmity, but a wounded spirit who can bear?
15 The heart of the prudent gets knowledge, and the ear of the wise seeks knowledge.
16 A man's gift makes room for him and brings him before great men.
17 *He that is* first in his own cause *seems* just, but his neighbor comes and searches him.
18 The lot causes contentions to cease and parts between the mighty.
19 A brother offended *is harder to be won* than a strong city, and *their* contentions *are* like the bars of a castle.
20 A man's belly shall be satisfied with the fruit of his mouth, *and* with the increase of his lips shall he be filled.
21 Death and life *are* in the power of the tongue, and they that love it shall eat the fruit thereof.
22 *Whoever* finds a wife finds a good *thing* and obtains favor of the LORD.
23 The poor use entreaties, but the rich answer roughly.
24 A man *that has* friends must show himself friendly, and there is a friend *that* sticks closer than a brother.

Chapter 19

1 Better *is* the poor that walks in his integrity than *he that is* perverse in his lips and is a fool.
2 Also, *it is* not good *that* the soul *be* without knowledge, and he that hastens with *his* feet sins.
3 The foolishness of a man perverts his way, and his heart frets against the LORD.
4 Wealth makes many friends, but the poor are separated from their neighbors.
5 A false witness shall not go unpunished, and *he that* speaks lies shall not escape.
6 Many will entreat the favor of the prince, and every man *is* a friend to him that gives gifts.
7 All the brethren of the poor hate him; how much more do his friends go far from him? He pursues *them with* words, *yet* they *ignore him.*
8 He that gets wisdom loves his own soul. He that keeps understanding shall find good.
9 A false witness shall not go unpunished, and *he that* speaks lies shall perish.

10 Delight is not seemly for a fool, much less for a servant to have rule over princes.
11 The discretion of a man defers his anger, and *it is* his glory to pass over a transgression.
12 The king's wrath *is* as the roaring of a lion, but his favor *is* as dew upon the grass.
13 A foolish son *is* the calamity of his father, and the contentions of a wife *are* a continual dropping.
14 House and riches *are* the inheritance of fathers, and a prudent wife *is* from the LORD.
15 Slothfulness casts into a deep sleep, and an idle soul shall suffer hunger.
16 He that keeps the commandment keeps his own soul, *but* he that despises his ways shall die.
17 He that has pity on the poor lends to the LORD, and that which he has given will He pay him again.
18 Chasten your son while there is hope and let not your soul spare for his crying.
19 A man of great wrath shall suffer punishment, and if you deliver *him*, you must do it again.
20 Hear counsel and receive instruction that you may be wise in your latter end.
21 *There are* many devices in a man's heart; nevertheless, the counsel of the LORD shall stand.
22 The desire of a man *is* his kindness, and a poor man *is* better than a liar.
23 The fear of the LORD *tends* to life, and *he that has it* shall abide satisfied; he shall not be visited with evil.
24 A slothful *man* hides his hand in *his* bosom and will not so much as bring it to his mouth again.
25 Smite a scorner, and the simple will beware. Reprove one that has understanding, *and* he will understand knowledge.

26 He that wastes *his* father *and* chases away *his* mother *is* a son that causes shame and brings reproach.
27 Cease, my son, to hear the instruction *that causes you* to stray from the words of knowledge.
28 An ungodly witness scorns judgment, and the mouth of the wicked devours iniquity.
29 Judgments are prepared for scorners and stripes for the backs of fools.

Chapter 20

1 Wine *is* a mocker, strong drink *is* raging, and whoever is deceived thereby is not wise.
2 The fear of a king *is* as the roaring of a lion; *whoever* provokes him to anger sins *against* his own soul.
3 *It is* an honor for a man to cease from strife, but every fool will be meddling.
4 The sluggard will not plow because of the cold; *therefore,* he shall beg in harvest and *have* nothing.
5 Counsel in the heart of man *is like* deep water, but a man of understanding will draw it out.
6 Most men will proclaim everyone his own goodness, but a faithful man who can find?
7 The just *man* walks in his integrity; his children *are* blessed after him.
8 A king that sits on the throne of judgment scatters away all evil with his eyes.
9 Who can say, I have made my heart clean, I am pure from my sin?
10 Diverse weights *and* measures are an abomination to the LORD.

11 Even a child is known by his doings, whether his work *is* pure and whether *it is* right.
12 The hearing ear and the seeing eye, the LORD made them both.
13 Love not sleep lest you come to poverty; open your eyes, *and* you shall be satisfied with bread.
14 *It is* naught, *it is* naught, says the buyer, but when he goes his way, then he boasts.
15 There is gold and a multitude of rubies, but the lips of knowledge *are* a precious jewel.
16 Take his garment that is surety *for* a stranger, and take a pledge of him for a strange woman.
17 Bread of deceit *is* sweet to a man but afterward his mouth will be filled with gravel.
18 *Every* purpose is established by counsel, and with good advice make war.
19 He that goes around *as* a talebearer reveals secrets; therefore, meddle not with him who flatters with his lips.
20 Whoever curses his father or his mother, his lamp shall be put out in obscure darkness.
21 An inheritance *may be* gotten hastily at the beginning, but the end thereof shall not be blessed.
22 Say not, I will recompense evil *but* wait on the LORD, and He will save you.
23 Diverse weights *are* an abomination unto the LORD, and a false balance *is* not good.
24 Man's goings *are* of the LORD; how can a man then understand his own way?
25 *It is* a snare to the man *who* devours *that which is* holy, and after vows to make inquiry.
26 A wise king scatters the wicked and brings the wheel over them.

27 The spirit of man *is* the candle of the LORD, searching all the inward parts of the belly.
28 Mercy and truth preserve the king, and his throne is upheld by mercy.
29 The glory of young men *is* their strength, and the beauty of old men *is* the gray head.
30 The blueness of a wound cleanses away evil, so *do* stripes the inward parts of the belly.

Chapter 21

1 The king's heart *is* in the hand of the LORD; *like* the rivers of water, He turns it whichever way He will.
2 Every way of a man *is* right in his own eyes, but the LORD ponders the heart.
3 To do justice and judgment *is* more acceptable to the LORD than sacrifice.
4 A high look, a proud heart, *and* the plowing of the wicked *is* sin.
5 The thoughts of the diligent *tend* only to plenteousness but of everyone *that is* hasty, only to want.
6 The getting of treasures by a lying tongue *is* a vanity tossed to and fro by them that seek death.
7 The robbery of the wicked shall destroy them because they refuse to do judgment.
8 The way of man *is* devious and strange, but *as for* the pure, his work *is* right.
9 *It is* better to dwell in a corner of the housetop than with a brawling woman in a wide house.
10 The soul of the wicked desires evil; his neighbor finds no favor in his eyes.

11 When the scorner is punished, the simple is made wise; and when the wise is instructed, he receives knowledge.
12 The righteous *man* wisely considers the house of the wicked, *but God* overthrows the wicked for *their* wickedness.
13 Whoever stops his ears at the cry of the poor, he will also cry himself, but shall not be heard.
14 A gift in secret pacifies anger and a reward in the bosom, strong wrath.
15 *It is* joy to the just to do judgment, but destruction *shall be* to the workers of iniquity.
16 The man that wanders out of the way of understanding shall remain in the congregation of the dead.
17 He that loves pleasure *shall be* a poor man; he that loves wine and oil shall not be rich.
18 The wicked *shall be* a ransom for the righteous and the transgressor for the upright.
19 *It is* better to dwell in the wilderness than with a contentious and angry woman.
20 *There is* treasure to be desired and oil in the dwelling of the wise, but a foolish man spends it up.
21 He that follows after righteousness and mercy finds life, righteousness, and honor.
22 A wise *man* scales the city of the mighty and casts down the strength of the confidence thereof.
23 Whoso keeps his mouth and his tongue keeps his soul from troubles.
24 Proud *and* haughty scorner *is* his name, who deals in proud wrath.
25 The desire of the slothful kills him, for his hands refuse to labor.
26 He covets greedily all day long, but the righteous gives and spares not.

27 The sacrifice of the wicked *is* an abomination; how much more, *when* he brings it with a wicked mind?
28 A false witness shall perish, but the man that hears, speaks constantly.
29 A wicked man hardens his face, but *as for* the upright, he directs his way.
30 *There is* no wisdom, nor understanding, nor counsel against the LORD.
31 The horse *is* prepared for the day of battle, but safety *is* from the LORD.

Chapter 22

1 A *good* name *is* rather to be chosen than great riches *and* loving favor rather than silver and gold.
2 The rich and the poor meet together; the LORD *is* the maker of them all.
3 A prudent *man* foresees the evil and hides himself, but the simple pass on and are punished.
4 By humility *and* the fear of the LORD *are* riches, honor, and life.
5 Thorns *and* snares *are* in the way of the perverse, but he that keeps his soul shall be far from them.
6 Train up a child in the way he should go, and when he is old, he will not depart from it.
7 The rich rule over the poor, and the borrower *is a servant* to the lender.
8 He that sows iniquity shall reap vanity, and the rod of his anger shall fail.
9 He that has a bountiful eye shall be blessed, for he gives of his bread to the poor.
10 Cast out the scorner and contention shall go out; yes, strife and reproach shall cease.

11 He that loves pureness of heart, *for* the grace of his lips, the king *shall be* his friend.
12 The eyes of the LORD preserve knowledge, and He overthrows the words of the transgressor.
13 The slothful *man* says, *there is* a lion outside, I shall be slain in the streets.
14 The mouths of strange women *are* a deep pit, and he that is abhorred by the LORD shall fall therein.
15 Foolishness *is* bound in the heart of a child, *but* the rod of correction shall drive it far from him.
16 He that oppresses the poor to increase his *riches, and* he that gives to the rich *shall* surely *come* to want.
17 Bow down your ear, hear the words of the wise, and apply your heart unto My knowledge.
18 For *it is* a pleasant thing if you keep them within you; they shall be fitted in your lips.
19 That your trust may be in the LORD, I have made known to you this day, even to you.
20 Have I not written to you excellent things in counsels and knowledge,
21 That I might make you know the certainty of the words of truth; that you might answer the words of truth to those who send unto you?
22 Rob not the poor because he *is* poor; neither oppress the afflicted in the gate.
23 For the LORD will plead their cause and spoil the soul of those that spoiled them.
24 Make no friendship with an angry man, and with a furious man you shall not go;
25 Lest you learn his ways and get a snare to your soul.
26 Be not *one* of them that strike hands nor of them that are sureties for debts.
27 If you have nothing to pay, why should he take away your bed from under you?

28 Remove not the ancient landmark which your fathers have set.

29 See a man diligent in his business? He shall stand before kings; he shall not stand before mean *men*.

Chapter 23

1 When you sit to eat with a ruler, consider diligently what *is* before you;
2 And put a knife to your throat if you *are* a man given to appetite.
3 Do not desire his dainties for they *are* deceitful food.
4 Labor not to be rich and cease from your own wisdom.
5 Will you set your eyes upon that which is not? For *riches* certainly make themselves wings, and they fly away as an eagle toward heaven.
6 Eat not the bread of *him that has* an evil eye, neither desire his dainty food;
7 For as he thinks in his heart, so *is* he. Eat and drink, he says to you, but his heart *is* not with you.
8 The morsel *which* you have eaten shall you vomit up and lose your sweet words.
9 Speak not in the ears of a fool, for he will despise the wisdom of your words.
10 Remove not the old landmark and enter not into the fields of the fatherless;

11 For their Redeemer *is* mighty, and He will plead their cause with you.
12 Apply your heart unto instruction and your ears to the words of knowledge.
13 Withhold not correction from the child, for *if* you beat him with the rod, he shall not die.
14 You shall beat him with the rod and deliver his soul from hell.
15 My son, if your heart is wise, my heart shall rejoice, even mine.
16 Yes, my heart shall rejoice when your lips say the right things.
17 Let not your heart envy sinners but fear the LORD all day long.
18 For surely there is an end, and your expectation shall not be cut off.
19 Hear my son, be wise and guide your heart in the way.
20 Be not among winebibbers and riotous eaters of flesh;
21 For the drunkard and the glutton shall come to poverty and drowsiness shall clothe *a man* with rags.
22 Listen to your father that begot you and despise not your mother when she is old.
23 Buy the truth and sell *it* not; *also,* wisdom, instruction, and understanding.
24 The father of the righteous shall greatly rejoice, and he that begets a wise *child* shall have joy of him.
25 Your father and your mother will be glad, and she that bore you shall rejoice.
26 My son, give me your heart and let your eyes observe my ways.
27 For a harlot *is* a deep ditch, and a strange woman *is* a narrow pit.
28 She lies in wait as *for* a prey and increases the transgressors among men.

29 Who has sadness? Who has sorrow? Who has contentions? Who has babbling? Who has wounds without cause? Who has redness of eyes?
30 Those who tarry long at the wine and those that seek mixed wine.
31 Look not upon the wine when it is red, when it gives its color in the cup, *when* it moves itself aright.
32 At the last, it bites like a serpent and stings like an adder.
33 Your eyes shall behold strange women, and your heart shall utter perverse things.
34 Yes, you shall be like he that lies down in the middle of the sea or like he that lies upon the top of a mast.
35 They have stricken me, *you will say, and* I was not sick; they have beaten me, *and* I felt *it* not. When will I awaken? I will seek it again.

Chapter 24

1 Be not envious of evil men, neither desire to be with them;
2 For their heart studies destruction, and their lips talk of mischief.
3 Through wisdom a house is built, by understanding it is established;
4 And by knowledge, the chambers shall be filled with all precious and pleasant riches.
5 A wise man *is* strong, yes, a man of knowledge increases strength.
6 By wise counsel you shall make your war, and in the multitude of counselors, *there is* safety.
7 Wisdom *is* too high for a fool; he opens not his mouth in the gate.
8 He that devises to do evil shall be called a mischievous person.
9 The thought of foolishness *is* sin, and the scorner *is* an abomination to men.
10 *If* you faint in the day of adversity, your strength *is* small.

11 If you don't deliver *them that are* drawn unto death and *those that are* ready to be slain;
12 If you say we knew it not, does not He that ponders the heart consider *it*? And He that keeps your soul, does He not know *it*? And shall He not render to *every* man according to his works?
13 My son, eat honey because *it is* good and the honeycomb, *which is* sweet to your taste;
14 So *shall* the knowledge of wisdom *be* to your soul; when you have found *it*, then there shall be a reward, and your expectation shall not be cut off.
15 Lay not waiting, O wicked *man*, against the dwelling of the righteous; spoil not his resting place;
16 For a just *man* falls seven times and rises again, but the wicked shall fall into mischief.
17 Rejoice not when your enemy falls and let not your heart be glad when he stumbles;
18 Lest the LORD see *it*, it displeases Him, and He turns away His wrath from him.
19 Fret not thyself because of evil *men*, neither be envious of the wicked;
20 For there shall be no reward to the evil *man*, and the candle of the wicked shall be put out.
21 My son, fear the LORD and the king, *and* meddle not with them that are given to change;
22 For their calamity shall rise suddenly, and who knows the ruin of them both?
23 These *things* also *belong* to the wise. *It is* not good to have respect of persons in judgment.
24 He that says to the wicked, you *are* righteous, the people will curse and nations shall abhor him;
25 But to those that rebuke *him* shall be delight, and a good blessing shall come upon them.
26 *Every man* shall kiss *the* lips that give a right answer.

27 Prepare you work without, make it fit for yourself in the field, and afterward build your house.
28 Be not a witness against your neighbor without cause and deceive *not* with your lips.
29 Say not, I will do unto him as he has done unto me; I will render to the man according to his work.
30 I went by the field of the slothful and by the vineyard of the man void of understanding;
31 And it was all overgrown with thorns, nettles had covered the face of it, and the stone wall was broken down.
32 Then I saw *and* considered *it* well. I looked upon *it and* received instruction.
33 *Yes*, a little sleep, a little slumber, a little folding of the hands to sleep;
34 So shall your poverty come *as* one that travels and your want as an armed man.

Chapter 25

1 These *are* also proverbs of Solomon, which the men of Hezekiah, king of Judah, copied out.
2 *It is* the glory of God to conceal a thing, but the honor of kings *is* to search out a matter.
3 The heaven for height, the earth for depth, and the hearts of kings *are* unsearchable.
4 Take away the dross from the silver and there shall come forth a vessel for the refiner.
5 Take away the wicked *from* before the king and his throne shall be established in righteousness.
6 Do not put yourself in the presence of the king and do not stand in the place of great *men*;
7 For *it is* better that it be said to you, come up here, than that you should be put lower in the presence of the prince, whom your eyes have seen.
8 Do not go hastily to strive, lest *you know not* what to do in the end, when your neighbor has put you to shame.
9 Debate your cause with your neighbor *privately* and divulge not a secret to another;

10 Lest he that hears *it* put you to shame and your infamy turn not away.
11 A word fitly spoken *is like* apples of gold in pictures of silver.
12 *As* an earring of gold, and an ornament of fine gold, *so is* a wise reprover upon an obedient ear.
13 As the cold of snow in the time of harvest, *so is* a faithful messenger to them that send him; for he refreshes the soul of his masters.
14 Whoever boasts himself of a false gift *is like* clouds and wind without rain.
15 By long forbearing is a prince persuaded, and a soft tongue breaks the bone.
16 Have you found honey? Eat as much is sufficient for you, lest you be filled therewith, and vomit it.
17 Withdraw your foot from your neighbor's house lest he be weary of you and hate you.
18 A man that bears false witness against his neighbor *is* a maul, a sword, and a sharp arrow.
19 Confidence in an unfaithful man, in times of trouble, *is like* a broken tooth and a foot out of joint.
20 *As* he that takes away a garment in cold weather *and as* vinegar upon soda, so *is* he that sings songs to a heavy heart.
21 If your enemy is hungry, give him bread to eat, and if he is thirsty, give him water to drink;
22 For you will heap coals of fire upon his head, and the LORD will reward you.
23 The north wind drives away rain, so *does* an angry countenance a backbiting tongue.
24 *It is* better to dwell in the corner of the housetop than with a brawling woman in a wide house.
25 *As* cold water to a thirsty soul, so *is* good news from a far away country.

26 A righteous man falling before the wicked *is like* a troubled fountain and a corrupt spring.
27 *It is* not good to eat too much honey, so *for men* to search their own glory, *is not* glory.
28 He that *has* no rule over his own spirit *is like* a city *that is* broken down without walls.

Chapter 26

1 As snow in summer and rain in harvest, so honor is not seemly for a fool.
2 As the bird by wandering, as the swallow by flying, so the causeless curse shall not come.
3 A whip for the horse, a bridle for the ass, and a rod for the fool's back.
4 Answer not a fool according to his folly, lest you also be like him.
5 Answer a fool according to his folly, lest he be wise in his own conceit.
6 He that sends a message by the hand of a fool cuts off the feet *and* drinks damage.
7 The legs of the lame are not equal, so *is* a parable in the mouth of fools.
8 As he that binds a stone in a sling, so *is* he that gives honor to a fool.
9 *As* a thorn goes up into the hand of a drunkard, so *is* a parable in the mouth of fools.
10 The great *God* that formed all *things* rewards both the fool and the transgressors.

11 As a dog returns to his vomit, *so* a fool returns to his folly.
12 See a man wise in his own conceit? *There is* more hope of a fool than of him.
13 The slothful *man* says, *there is* a lion in the way; a lion *is* in the streets.
14 *As* the door turns upon its hinges, so *does* the slothful upon his bed.
15 The slothful hides his hand in *his* bosom; it grieves him to bring it to his mouth again.
16 The sluggard *is* wiser in his own conceit than seven men that can render a reason.
17 He that passes by *and* meddles with strife, not *belonging* to him, *is like* one that takes a dog by the ears.
18 As a mad *man* who casts firebrands, arrows and death;
19 So *is* the man *that* deceives his neighbor and says, am I not in sport?
20 Where no wood is, the fire goes out; so, where *there is* no talebearer, the strife ceases.
21 *As* coals *are* to burning coals, and wood to fire, so *is* a contentious man to kindle strife.
22 The words of a talebearer *are* as wounds, and they go down into the innermost parts of the belly.
23 Burning lips and a wicked heart *are like* broken pottery covered with silver dross.
24 He that hates dissembles with his lips and lays up deceit within himself.
25 When he speaks pleasantly, believe him not, for *there are* seven abominations in his heart;
26 *Whose* hatred is covered by deceit; his wickedness shall be shown before the *whole* congregation.
27 Whoever digs a pit shall fall therein, and he that rolls a stone, it will return upon him.

28 A lying tongue hates *those that are* afflicted by it, and a flattering mouth works ruin.

Chapter 27

1 Boast not about tomorrow, for you know not what a day may bring forth.
2 Let another man praise you, and not your own mouth, a stranger and not your own lips.
3 A stone *is* heavy, and the sand weighty, but a fool's wrath *is* heavier than them both.
4 Wrath *is* cruel and anger *is* outrageous, but who *is* able to stand before envy?
5 Open rebuke *is* better than secret love.
6 Faithful *are* the wounds of a friend, but the kisses of an enemy *are* deceitful.
7 The full soul loathes a honeycomb, but to the hungry soul, every bitter thing is sweet.
8 As a bird that wanders from her nest, so *is* a man that wanders from his place.
9 Ointment and perfume rejoice the heart; so *does* the sweetness of a man's friend by hearty counsel.
10 Your own friend and your father's friend, forsake not; neither go into your brother's house in the day of thy

calamity; *for* better *is* a neighbor *that is* near than a brother far off.

11 My son, be wise and make my heart glad, that I may answer him that reproaches me.

12 A prudent *man* foresees the evil *and* hides himself, *but* the simple pass on and are punished.

13 Take his garment that is surety for a stranger and take a pledge of him for a strange woman.

14 He that blesses his friend with a loud voice, rising early in the morning, it shall be counted a curse to him.

15 A continual dropping, in a very rainy day, and a contentious woman are alike;

16 Whoever hides her hides the wind and the ointment of his right hand will betray *him*.

17 Iron sharpens iron, so a man sharpens the countenance of his friend.

18 Whoever keeps the fig tree shall eat the fruit, so he that waits on his master shall be honored.

19 As in water, face *answers* to face, so the heart of man to man.

20 Hell and destruction are never full, so the eyes of man are never satisfied.

21 *As* the fining pot for silver, and the furnace for gold, so *is* a man to his praise.

22 Though you crush a fool in a mortar, among wheat with a pestle, *yet* his foolishness will not depart from him.

23 Be diligent to know the state of your flocks *and* look well to your herds.

24 For riches *are* not forever, and does the crown *endure* to every generation?

25 The hay appears, the tender grass shows itself, and the herbs of the mountains are gathered.

26 The lambs *are* for your clothing; the goats *are* the price of the field;

27 And *you shall have* enough goats' milk for your food, for the food of your household, and *for* the maintenance of your maidens.

Chapter 28

1 The wicked flee when no man pursues, but the righteous are bold as a lion.
2 For the transgression of a land, many *are* the princes thereof, but by a man of understanding *and* knowledge, the state *thereof* shall be prolonged.
3 A poor man that oppresses the poor *is like* a sweeping rain which leaves no food.
4 They that forsake the law praise the wicked, but those who keep the law contend with them.
5 Evil men understand not judgment, but they that seek the LORD understand all *things*.
6 Better *is* the poor that walks in his uprightness than *he that is* rich and perverse *in his* ways.
7 Whoever keeps the law *is* a wise son, but he who is a companion of riotous *men* shames his father.
8 He that by usury and unjust gain increases his substance, shall gather it for him that will pity the poor.
9 He that turns away his ear from hearing the law, even his prayer *shall be* an abomination.
10 Whoever causes the righteous to go astray in an evil

way shall fall into his own pit, but the upright shall have good *things* in possession.
11 The rich man *is* wise in his own conceit, but the poor that has understanding searches him out.
12 When righteous *men* rejoice, *there is* great glory; but when the wicked rise, a man is hidden.
13 He that covers his sins shall not prosper, but whoever confesses and forsakes *them* shall have mercy.
14 Happy *is* the man that fears always, but he that hardens his heart shall fall into mischief.
15 *As* a roaring lion and a ranging bear, *so is* a wicked ruler over the poor.
16 The prince that lacks understanding *is* also a great oppressor, *but* he that hates covetousness shall prolong *his* days.
17 A man that does violence to the blood of *any* person shall flee to the pit; let no man sustain him.
18 Whoso walks uprightly shall be saved but *he that is* perverse *in his* ways shall fall at once.
19 He that tills his land shall have plenty of bread, but he that follows vain *persons* shall have poverty enough.
20 A faithful man shall abound with blessings, but he that makes haste to be rich shall not be innocent.
21 Having respect of persons *is* not good because for a piece of bread *that* man will transgress.
22 He that hastens to be rich *has* an evil eye and considers not that poverty shall come upon him.
23 He that rebukes a man afterward shall find more favor than he that flatters with the tongue.
24 Whoever robs his father or his mother and says *it is* no transgression; the same *is* the companion of a destroyer.
25 He that has a proud heart stirs up strife, but he that puts his trust in the LORD shall be made fat.

26 He that trusts in his own heart is a fool, but whoever walks wisely shall be delivered.
27 He that gives to the poor shall not lack, but he that hides his eyes shall have many curses.
28 When the wicked rise, men hide themselves, but when they perish, the righteous increase.

Chapter 29

1 He that is often reproved hardens *his* neck and shall suddenly be destroyed without remedy.
2 When the righteous are in authority, the people rejoice, but when the wicked rule, the people mourn.
3 Whoever loves wisdom rejoices his father, but he that keeps company with harlots spends *his* substance.
4 The king by judgment establishes the land, but he that receives gifts overthrows it.
5 A man that flatters his neighbor spreads a net for his feet.
6 In the transgression of an evil man there *is* a snare, but the righteous sing and rejoice.
7 The righteous consider the cause of the poor, *but* the wicked prefer not to know *it*.
8 Scornful men bring a city into a snare, but wise *men* turn away wrath.
9 *If* a wise man contends with a foolish man, whether he rages or laughs, *there is* no rest.
10 The bloodthirsty hate the upright, but the just seek his soul.

11 A fool utters all his mind, but a wise *man* keeps it in till afterwards.
12 If a ruler harkens to lies, all his servants *are* wicked.
13 The poor and the deceitful man meet together; the LORD lightens both their eyes.
14 The king that faithfully judges the poor, his throne shall be established forever.
15 The rod and reproof give wisdom, but a child left *to himself* brings his mother to shame.
16 When the wicked are multiplied, transgression increases, but the righteous shall see their fall.
17 Correct your son and he will give you rest; yes, he will delight your soul.
18 Where *there is* no vision, the people perish, but he that keeps the law is happy.
19 A servant cannot be corrected by words, for though he understands, he will not answer.
20 Do you see a man *that is* hasty in his words? *There is* more hope of a fool than of him.
21 He that delicately brings up his servant from a child, shall have him become *his* son at the length.
22 An angry man stirs up strife, and a furious man abounds in transgression.
23 A man's pride will bring him low, but honor will uphold the humble in spirit.
24 Whoever is partner with a thief hates his own soul; he hears cursing and does not condemn it.
25 The fear of man brings a snare, but whoever puts his trust in the LORD shall be safe.
26 Many seek the ruler's favor, but *every* man's judgment *comes* from the LORD.
27 An unjust man *is* an abomination to the just, and *he that is* upright in the way *is* an abomination to the wicked.

Chapter 30

1 The words of Agur the son of Jakeh, *even* the prophecy. The man spoke unto Ithiel, even unto Ithiel and Ucal.
2 Surely, I *am* dumber than *any* man and have not the understanding of a man.
3 I neither learned wisdom nor have the knowledge of the Holy One.
4 Who has ascended up into heaven, or descended? Who has gathered the wind in His fists? Who has bound the waters in a garment? Who has established all the ends of the earth? What *is* His name, and what *is* His Son's name, if you can tell?
5 Every word of God *is* pure; He *is* a shield to them that put their trust in Him.
6 Do not add to His words, lest He reprove you and you are found to be a liar.
7 Two *things* I have required of you; do not deny them to me before I die.
8 Remove vanity and lies far from me, give me neither poverty nor riches, and feed me with food convenient for me;

9 Lest I be full, deny *you*, and say, who *is* the LORD? Or lest I be poor, steal, and take the name of my God *in vain*.
10 Accuse not a servant to his master, lest he curse you, and you be found guilty.
11 *There is* a generation *that* curses their father and does not bless their mother.
12 *There is* a generation *that is* pure in their own eyes and *yet* is not washed from their filthiness.
13 *There is* a generation, O how lofty are their eyes! And their eyelids are lifted up.
14 *There is* a generation whose teeth *are as* swords and their jaw teeth *as* knives, to devour the poor from off the earth and the needy from *among* men.
15 The horseleech has two daughters, *crying*, "Give, give." There are three *things that* are never satisfied, *yes*, four *things* say not, *it is* enough;
16 The grave, the barren womb, the earth *that* is not filled with water, and the fire *that* says not, *it is* enough.
17 The eye *that* mocks at *his* father and despises to obey *his* mother, the ravens of the valley will pick it out, and the young eagles shall eat it.
18 There are three *things which* are too wonderful for me, yes, four which I know not;
19 The way of an eagle in the air, the way of a serpent upon a rock, the way of a ship in the midst of the sea, and the way of a man with a maid.
20 Such *is* the way of an adulterous woman; she eats, wipes her mouth, and says, I have done no wickedness.
21 For three *things* the earth is disquieted and for four *which* it cannot bear:
22 For a servant when he reigns, a fool when he is filled with food,

23 For an odious *woman* when she is married, and a handmaid that is heir to her mistress.
24 There are four *things which are* little upon the earth, but they *are* exceedingly wise.
25 The ants *are* a people not strong, yet they prepare their food in the summer.
26 The conies *are* feeble folk, yet they make their houses in the rocks.
27 The locusts have no king, yet all of them go forth by bands.
28 The spider takes hold with her hands and is in kings' palaces.
29 There are three *things* which go well, yes, four are comely in going;
30 A lion *which is* strongest among beasts and turns not away for any,
31 A greyhound, a he goat also, and a king, against whom *there is* no rising up.
32 If you have done foolishly in lifting up yourself, or if you have thought evil, *put* your hand over your mouth.
33 Surely the churning of milk produces butter, and the wringing of the nose produces blood; so the forcing of wrath brings forth strife.

Chapter 31

1 These are the words of King Lemuel, the prophecy that his mother taught him.
2 What, my son? And what, the son of my womb? And what, the son of my vows?
3 Give not your strength to women, nor your ways to that which destroys kings.
4 *It is* not for kings, O Lemuel, *it is* not for kings to drink wine, nor for princes strong drink;
5 Lest they drink, forget the law, and pervert the judgment of any of the afflicted.
6 Give strong drink to him that is ready to perish and wine to those with a heavy heart.
7 Let him drink, forget his poverty, and remember his misery no more.
8 Open your mouth for the dumb, in the cause of all, who are appointed to destruction.
9 Open your mouth, judge righteously, and plead the cause of the poor and needy.
10 Who can find a virtuous woman? For her price *is* far above rubies.

11 The heart of her husband safely trusts in her so that he shall have no need of spoil.
12 She will do him good and not evil all the days of her life.
13 She seeks wool and flax and works willingly with her hands.
14 She is like the merchants' ships; she brings her food from afar.
15 She rises while it is still night, gives meat to her household and a portion to her maidens.
16 She considers a field and buys it; with the fruit of her hands, she plants a vineyard.
17 She girds her loins with strength and strengthens her arms.
18 She perceives that her merchandise *is* good; her candle does not go out at night.
19 She puts her hands on the spindle, and her hands hold the distaff.
20 She stretches out her hand to the poor; yes, she reaches her hands out to the needy.
21 She is not afraid of the snow for her household, for all of her household *are* clothed with scarlet.
22 She makes herself coverings of tapestry; her clothing *is* silk and purple.
23 Her husband is known in the gates when he sits among the elders of the land.
24 She makes fine linen, sells *it*, and delivers girdles to the merchant.
25 Strength and honor *are* her clothing, and she shall rejoice in time to come.
26 She opens her mouth with wisdom, and in her tongue *is* the law of kindness.
27 She looks well to the ways of her household and eats not the bread of idleness.

28 Her children arise up and call her blessed; her husband *also*, and he praises her.
29 Many daughters have done virtuously, but you excel them all.
30 Favor *is* deceitful, and beauty *is* vain, *but* a woman *that* fears the LORD, she shall be praised.
31 Give her of the fruit of her hands and let her own works praise her in the gates.

Part Two
Three Simple Steps

If you suddenly died today, are you absolutely sure where you'd spend eternity? If not, and you'd like to be sure, follow these simple ABCs:

A—**Admit** that you are a sinner.

"As it is written, there is none righteous, no, not one." (Rom. 3:10)

"For all have sinned and come short of the glory of God." (Rom. 3:23)

"For the wages of sin is death; but the gift of God is eternal life through Jesus Christ our Lord." (Rom. 6:23)

B—**Believe** in the Lord Jesus Christ.

"Believe in the Lord Jesus Christ and thou shalt be saved." (Acts 16:31)

"For God so loved the world, that He gave his only begotten Son, that whosoever believeth in Him, should not perish but have everlasting life." (John 3:16)

C—**Confess**

"If you confess with your mouth that Jesus is Lord and believe in your heart that God raised Him from the dead, you shall be saved." (Rom. 10:9)

"Jesus said, 'I am the way, the truth and the life; no man comes to the Father but by me.'" (John 14:6)

Now, pray this simple prayer:

> *Dear Jesus, I know I'm a sinner and deserve to die for my sins, but I believe that you came to earth and died for my sins that I might have eternal life. Jesus, will you please forgive me for my sins, come into my heart, and be the Lord of my life? Amen.*

If you prayed this simple prayer, we would love to hear from you and hear your story.

Please email us at:

TheBookofProverbs333@gmail.com

Part Three
Final Thoughts

WHAT SHOULD YOU DO NOW?

Tell someone about your decision, find a church that teaches the Bible, learn about the Life of Jesus, and read the Bible daily.

WHERE SHOULD YOU START READING?

The four Gospels—Matthew, Mark, Luke, and John—were written by four of Jesus's closest apostles. Each of these books recount His life, the miracles He performed, His instructions on how to live in the world, His death, and His resurrection. Some say it's best to read the book of John first followed by Matthew, Mark, and Luke. Wherever you decide to start reading, ask God to speak to you through His Word, and He will. Remember, prayer is us speaking to God, and the Bible is God speaking to us.

Blessings!

DrG